WELCOME TO MELROSE ABBEY

Melrose Abbey, at the heart of the Scottish Border country, was founded in 1136 by Cistercian monks.

These monks aspired to live by an austere set of monastic principles. At Melrose they found fertile land by the River Tweed, already holy in connection with the early saints, St Aidan and St Cuthbert. The abbey would become one of the wealthiest monasteries in medieval Scotland, and its abbey church is one of the finest expressions of the order's 'architecture of solitude'.

As you explore the abbey ruins, look for the exquisite fineness of detail created by the medieval masons over centuries of work and worship.

Right: An illustration for Sir Walter Scott's 'The Lay of the Last Minstrel', by J.M.W. Turner.

Opposite: A view into the monks' cloister from the south transept.

CONTENTS

HIGHLIGHTS   2

EXPLORE   4

At a glance	4
The abbey church	6
The nave	8
The aisle chapels	10
The monks' choir	12
The transepts	14
The presbytery	16
The church exterior	18
The chapter house	22
The domestic buildings	24
A heavenly place	28

HISTORY   30

Old Melrose	32
The Cistercians	34
David I's abbey	36
Monastic life at Melrose	38
The Wars of Independence	40
A phoenix from the ashes	42
Decline and fall	44
'Far-fam'd glorious ruins'	46

DISCOVER HISTORIC SCOTLAND	49
HISTORIC SCOTLAND MEMBERSHIP	49
FURTHER READING	49

HIGHLIGHTS

▲ **A HOUSE OF HOLY MEN**
Melrose was a holy place very early in Scotland's Christian history. Chroniclers tell of miracles here, concerning the saints Aidan, Boisil and Cuthbert. Later, the miracles of St Waltheof continued to draw pilgrims to Melrose (p.32–33).

▲ **ROBERT THE BRUCE**
Though the king was buried at Dunfermline, his heart was interred at Melrose, after it had been taken to Spain on crusade (p.40–41).

▲ **THE BAGPIPE-PLAYING PIG**
This famous carving may be an expression of medieval humour. Bagpipes were often used to evoke parts of the male anatomy, and pigs were thought of as unclean animals (p.18).

▲ EVERYDAY OBJECTS
These urinals were found in the main drain
that flushed the monks' toilets (p.24–25).

▲ HEAVENLY MUSE
Many artists and writers visited the abbey, and were inspired by the rose-coloured ruin.
Sir Walter Scott lived nearby, and based several of his tales in the vicinity (p.46–47).

▲ CARVED CREATIONS
Demons vie with lute-playing angels for space
on the exterior walls of the church (p.18–21).

▲ A PEACEFUL PLACE
The abbey lies low in a verdant valley, a line of hills circling the horizon (p.28–29).

AT A GLANCE

The abbey church at Melrose was first built in the 1100s, but was largely destroyed by Richard II's English army in 1385. Many of the buildings we see date from the period of rebuilding which followed.

At Melrose, the abbey precinct was particularly large, and would have been a hive of industry. Until the 1400s, most of the manual labour was undertaken by lay brothers – men who took monastic vows but who were not ordained as priests. They were generally illiterate and usually entered the order later in life. They lived in their own cloister, and worshipped in a part of the abbey church separate from the monks.

1 GALILEE PORCH
The entrance to the church added in the later 1100s. You can still see parts of column bases that supported its vaulted ceiling.

2 NAVE
Where the lay brothers worshipped until the 1400s.

3 AISLE CHAPELS
Small chapels, often used as burial places by wealthy locals.

4 MONKS' CHOIR
Where the monks sat during their services.

5 TRANSEPTS
The 'arms' of this cross-shaped church.

6 PRESBYTERY
Containing the high altar, this was the holiest part of the church.

7 SACRISTY
A store for the abbey's vestments and vessels, where monks dressed for services.

8 CHAPTER HOUSE
A meeting room, where abbey business would be conducted and a chapter of the monastic rule read each day.

9 LATRINE
The abbey toilets, or 'reredorter', flushed by the great drain.

10 CLOISTER
A central garth or square, around which the main abbey buildings were arranged.

11 WASH PLACE
The 'lavatorium', where monks washed their hands before meals.

- ■ 12-13th Century
- ■ 1385-1590
- ■ 1618
- ■ Modern

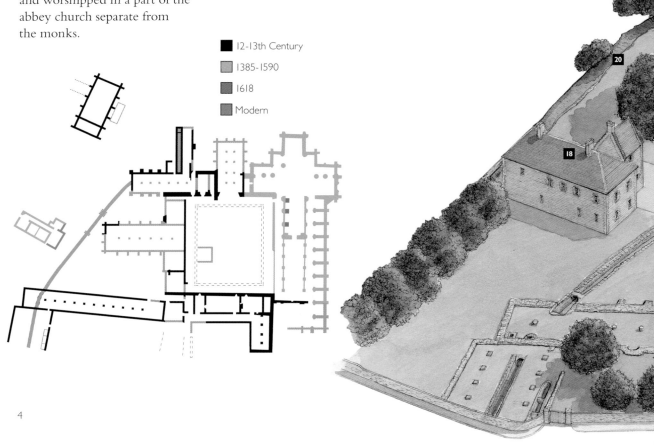

12 NOVICE'S DAY ROOM
Where the novice monks could work and learn about monastic life.

13 WARMING ROOM
A room in which monks were allowed to warm themselves for short periods each day.

14 REFECTORY
The abbey dining hall.

15 KITCHEN
Where meals were prepared for the community.

16 LAY BROTHERS' RANGE
Where the labour force of the Cistercians lived and worked.

17 MAIN DRAIN
A channel which washed waste away from the abbey.

18 COMMENDATOR'S HOUSE
Built in the 1400s for an unknown purpose, in 1590 this building was converted into the house of Commendator James Douglas.

19 ABBOT'S HALL
A large hall, probably built by Abbot Matthew in 1246.

20 MILL-LADE
Diverted from the River Tweed to power the abbey's mills and industry.

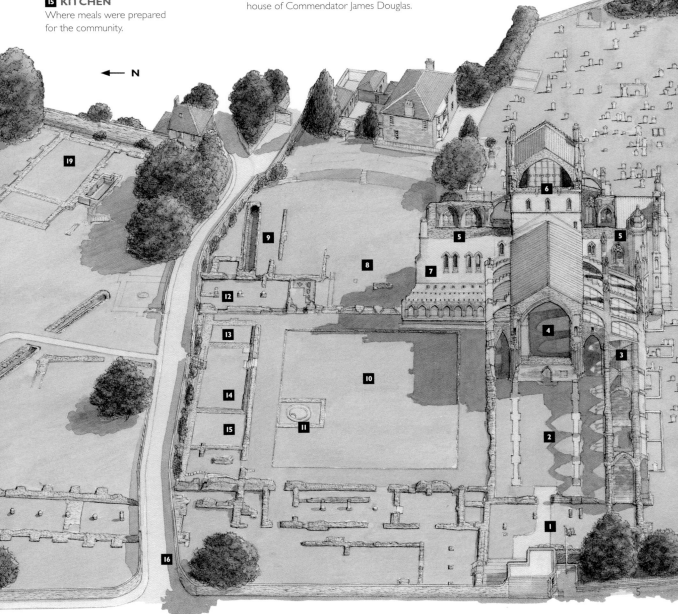

THE ABBEY CHURCH

The abbey church lay at the heart of the monastic community – and its high altar was the focus of worship.

In the church, the monastic community worshipped daily. The monks performed an almost constant round of services in the choir, guided by the strict Rule of St Benedict. On a winter's day, a Cistercian monk might rise at 2.30am for Nocturns – the day's first prayers, after which they would stay awake to read. Their next office would be Matins at daybreak, around 6am. This would be followed by reading and Prime. At 8am they would wash and change into day shoes. The prayer service of Terce would be followed by spoken Mass. At 9am the monks would meet in the Chapter House. Daily tasks would be assigned and work undertaken.

Right: Column bases surviving from the 'Galilee Porch', dating to the later 1100s. The porch formed part of the church's original west front.

Opposite: The great crossing of Melrose abbey church, looking towards the presbytery and north transept.

At noon, the service of Sext would be followed by a sung Mass, and None prayers at 1.30pm. Dinner, or Prandium, at 2pm would precede more work. At 4.15pm prayers were said at Vespers. From 5.30pm, monks could change into their night shoes, and have an evening drink. A short reading, or Collatio, would be followed by prayers at Compline, before retiring to bed at 6.30pm in a communal dormitory.

The church the monks worshipped in changed a great deal over the centuries. The early church, built in the 1100s, would have been a simple, largely unadorned building.

It was devastated by the attack of 1385, and was rebuilt to a similar floorplan, but on a much larger scale. The rose-tinted and buff-coloured sandstones were quarried from the nearby Eildon Hills. The transepts and presbytery were enlarged and extended further east. A series of chapels was added down one side of the nave.

The magnificent ruins we see today testify to the ambitions of the church's builders. However, the planned western part of the nave was probably never completed and the original front was never entirely demolished.

THE NAVE

The church was divided into different spaces, each used by different parts of the community. From the 1100s to 1385, the lay brothers worshipped in the western part of the nave, separated from the monks' choir to the east.

The lay brothers would have sat ranged in choir stalls, like the monks in their choir beyond. The space would have had unadorned, whitewashed walls, and only the simplest of furnishings – choir stalls and a wooden cross.

The only part of this church which survives today is a fragment of the west wall. The location of the entrance doorway can still be seen, as well as column bases, which once formed part of a 'Galilee' porch dating to the later 1100s. There monks assembled for their Sunday procession.

After the destruction of 1385, rebuilding began on this end of the church. However, lay brothers were no longer being recruited to the Cistercian order by the 1400s. It is likely that this made the need to complete the nave less urgent, and that the planned building was never finished.

Today, only traces remain to give clues to how this space originally looked.

Opposite: The lay-brothers' nave as it may have looked in the early 1200s. The buildings are simple and unadorned, in line with the Cistercian order's austere code.

There are a number of burials, and fragments of grave-covers survive. The grand aisle chapels down one side of the nave show the scale envisaged by those rebuilding the church after 1385.

THE AISLE CHAPELS

After 1385, grand aisle chapels were built down one side of the church. Eight survive today.

Wooden screens created enclosed chapels in the aisles. In each one, there would have been an altar, furnished with a decorative altar piece, or retable. By the altar a basin, or *piscina*, was used to rinse holy vessels. The insides of the basins are scalloped or plain, and the outsides ornamented with a leaf pattern. On either side of most of the basins are niches. These held cruets for the bread and water used in Holy Communion.

The three westernmost chapels, off the nave, were the last to be completed, in the time of Abbot William Turnbull (1503–06). His initials can faintly be seen by the piscina in the third chapel from the west. This chapel also contains a grave-slab, which once bore the figure of a man and the inscription 'Here lies an honourable man George Haliburton (who died 1 October 1538)'.

The fourth chapel (from the west) may have been dedicated to St Michael – his image adorns the central boss of the vaulting. On another boss, an angel holds the decayed arms of Abbot Andrew Hunter (1444-65). This chapel became the burial-place of the Pringles of Woodhouse and Whytebank. The epitaph of Christine Lundie, laid to rest in this chapel, reads:

HEIR LIES ANE HO/NORA[BIL VO]MAN CRISTIN LVNDIE / SPOVS TO IAM[ES PRINGIL OF] QVHYTBANK SCHO DECEIS / SIT 19 JVLY 1602 / LAMENT FOR / SYN AND STYL THOV MVRN / FOR TO THE CL / AY [ALL] VE MEN TVRN.

This translates as
'Here lies an honourable woman, Christine Lundie, spouse to James Pringle of Whytebank, who deceased 19 July 1602. Lament for that time and still thou mourn, for to the clay all ye must turn."

The Scotts of Gala and the Pringles of Galashiels were buried in the fifth chapel. It contains an effigy of Andrew Pringle, who lived at Smailholm Tower and died in 1585. The sixth chapel has a monument to David Fletcher, minister of Melrose and later bishop of Argyll. He died in 1665. Set into the floor of the eighth chapel is a tomb dating to the 1200s, of prayer-desk form. The inscription on its sloping top reads:

ORATE PRO / ANIMA FRATRIS PETRI CEL[L]ARII

'Pray for the soul of Brother Peter, the cellarer'.

Below: A view across the nave to the aisle chapels beyond. They ran almost the whole length of the church, though these western ones may never have been completed.

Opposite: An artist's impression of a monk praying in one of the aisle chapels around 1400.

THE MONKS' CHOIR

The monks worshipped in their choir, east of the great screen which divided the church. Separated from the lay brothers, they sang, chanted and read services here throughout the day. Further east lay the presbytery, and the high altar.

In the choir there would have been rows of choir stalls. Their hinged seats lifted up, and on the seats' lower sides were ledges, known as *misericords*, or mercy seats, against which the monks could rest during long periods standing. We know that stalls were ordered from Cornelius de Aeltre of Bruges in the 1430s.

Below: Finely carved foliage on the choir columns.

Opposite: An artist's impression of monks chanting in the choir around 1400.

The order was very specific, stipulating that the general design should be based on stalls at the abbey of Ten Duinen in Flanders, and that the carving should be like those at Ter Duinen and Ter Doest, near Bruges. These abbeys were centres of Flemish artistry, and the monks of Melrose were aiming very high. Sadly, nothing remains of the choir stalls today, and we can only imagine the lavish decoration that would have adorned this space. Hints of finery remain – look at the top of the columns in this part of the church, beautifully carved with leaf ornament.

After the Protestant Reformation of 1560, worship in this part of the church changed dramatically.

In the early 1600s it was adapted for use as a parish church. It is likely that the vaulting here had never been finished, so massive stone columns were built on the north side to support the roof. They carried a plain stone vault. Walls with windows were erected at either end. The interior was fitted out with galleries – the joist holes for these can still be seen. The space, once reserved for the monks, was now open for public worship.

In 1810, a new parish church was built in the town, and the one here in the abbey fell out of use. The end walls were taken down, leaving the structure as it appears today.

THE TRANSEPTS

The transepts are the two 'arms' of this cross-shaped church, either side of the central crossing.

In each transept there were eastern chapels, which housed altars where the monks offered up private prayers for the souls of their patrons. Each chapel had an altar under the east window. The chapels in the north transept were dedicated to St Peter and St Paul; their statues stand beneath canopies in niches high up on the west wall of the transept. The chapels either side of the presbytery were dedicated to St Benedict to the north and possibly St Martin to the south. The dedications of the south transept chapels are not known.

In the north transept, a wide stone stair once connected the church to the monks' dormitory, allowing the monks easy access for night-time services.

At the foot of the stair, we can still see a holy water 'stoup', or basin, where monks would ritually cleanse themselves on entering the church.

A door in the north transept led into the sacristy, where the altar vestments and vessels were kept; it was described as a 'wax cellar' in 1558. High above the doorway is a long, sunken panel which was probably decorated with images of metal or wood set on the 14 large and 14 small stone pedestals. Above this are three arched openings into the clerestory passage, and over all is a circular window with its finely carved tracery still complete.

In the south transept are two interesting inscriptions. Both refer to a Parisian born master-mason called John Morow, who worked here around 1400.

On one panel, Morow seems to have dictated his own epitaph:

[IOHN MOROW SUM TY]M CALLIT [WAS I AND BORN] IN PARYSSE / [CERTANLY AND HAD] IN KEPYING / [AL MASON WERK] OF SANTAN / [DROYS YE HYE K]YRK OF GLAS / GW MELROS AND] PASLAY OF / [NYDDYSDAYLL AND OF] GLAWAY / [I PRAY TO GOD AND MAR]I BATHE / [& SWETE SANCT IOHNE TO KEPE / THIS HALY KYRK FRA SKATHE].

John Morow sometimes called was I and born in Paris certainly and had in keeping all the mason work of St Andrews, the high kirk of Glasgow, Melrose and Paisley, of Nithsdale and Galloway. I pray to God and Mary both and sweet St John to keep this holy church from harm.'

A second panel reads, 'As the compass goes evenly about, so truth and loyalty shall do without doubt. Look to the end quoth John Morow.'

Left: The original John Morow inscription, on display in the Commendator's House. The one in the south transept is a replica.

Opposite: The north transept. The door set high in the wall led into the monks' dormitory.

THE PRESBYTERY

The presbytery, at the easternmost end of the church, housed the high altar. It was lit from three sides by magnificent windows.

Many traces of how this part of the church was used for medieval monastic worship survive today. The builders of later-medieval churches tended to 'build in' furnishings in stone, and it is this which has secured their survival. More portable furnishings would have been destroyed after the Protestant Reformation of 1560.

Under the east window there are two wall-cupboards. It is possible that these once held holy relics, of which Melrose Abbey amassed a collection. The elaborate reliquaries and their precious contents would have been locked safely away in the cupboards here, close to the high altar.

The relics acted as a focus for pilgrimage, and would have attracted many people to Melrose. They would only have been displayed during important celebrations.

In the south wall there is a tomb recess and two finely carved recesses. The left-hand one would have been a credence, which held the bread, wine and water used in Holy Communion, while the right-hand one was a double *piscina*, or basin, where the sacred vessels and the priest's hands could be washed.

The north wall also houses a tomb recess. Though it was officially forbidden for laymen to be buried in Cistercian churches, the rule was relaxed and the presbytery became a high-status burial place for society's elite; Alexander II was interred here in 1249.

Robert the Bruce's heart was probably also laid to rest here in 1331.

An intricate pattern of ribs and bosses adorns the stone vault over the presbytery. The central boss, positioned directly over the high altar, represents the Holy Trinity, attended by two angels. To the west is St Andrew holding his cross, and reading clockwise are: St Bartholomew holding the flaying knife, St Peter with the keys, St Thomas with the spear, St James the Less grasping the bludgeon, St James the Greater holding his staff and a scrip (a pilgrim's bag) or costrel (a leather-covered flask), St Paul with a sword, and St Matthias with an axe. To the south of St Andrew is a saint holding a book. One boss shows an angel, and others are carved with roses and leaves.

Above: The presbytery's credence and double *piscina*.

Right: Interconnected ribs and depictions of saints adorn the vaulted ceiling over the site of the high altar.

Opposite: The presbytery viewed from the crossing. It was the holiest part of the church, around the high altar.

THE CHURCH EXTERIOR

The doorway in the south transept leads to the graveyard beside the abbey church. This was the final resting-place of monks, before becoming the parish burial ground. From here you can see some of the beautiful carvings which survive on the walls of the church.

The exterior of the church at Melrose was lavishly carved with beasts, saints and sinners. Although many of the statues are missing, what remains is still one of the most stunning collections of medieval carving surviving in Scotland.

There are flying dragons that belched out roof-water, demons on the buttresses, beautiful images of Christ, the Virgin Mary, saints and martyrs in elaborate niches, angelic musicians on projecting corbels, and heads of kings, queens, lords, ladies, monks, craftsmen and crones looking down from their places by the abbey windows.

Some of the carvings may seem irreverent to us today – strange choices for a place of spiritual contemplation. But medieval people believed that animals were created by God to instruct humanity.

Everything in the natural world had a moral lesson to impart. Some of the carvings depict recognisable animals – like Melrose's famous bagpipe-playing pig – while others are conjured from the realms of myth and imagination. Medieval people drew no distinction. By picturing something, it could be made flesh.

The south transept is one of the most highly adorned parts of the church. Its exterior is dominated by niches with canopies at the top and carved corbels at the bottom. The corbels are carved with bearded men holding labels.

A figure on the west buttress holds a label extolling us to TIMET[E] DEU[M], 'fear the Lord'. Another scroll hopefully declares CU[M] VEN[IT] JES[US] SEQ[UAX?] CESSABIT [UMBRA], 'When Jesus comes the shadow will cease'. A third states PASSUS E[ST] Q[UIA] IP[S]E VOLUIT, 'He suffered because He himself willed it'.

Above the doorway into the south transept, a shield bears the royal arms. On either side stand figures, now headless: St Andrew, St Peter, a kneeling figure with hands clasped, a kneeling figure holding a book, St Paul and St Thomas.

In the centre of the group a bearded man holds a scroll declaring ECCE FILIUS DEI, 'Behold the Son of God'.

Above the great window, an elaborate niche probably contained a seated figure of the Virgin Mary. The belfry at the top of the gable was built for the post-Reformation kirk. Its Dutch bell survives with the inscription, IAN BURGERHVYS ME FECIT 1608, 'Jan Burgerhuys made me 1608'.

Corbels on the walls of the eastern chapels are carved to show a monk with his rosary beads, angels with curly hair playing musical instruments, a cook with a ladle, and a mason with his chisel and mell (mallet).

Opposite: A pageant of carvings on the exterior of the south transept.

Below: Two carved figures. Their scrolls carry moral and religious teachings.

THE CHURCH EXTERIOR (CONTINUED)

The pageant of carving continues on the exterior walls of the presbytery and the aisle chapels.

The east wall of the presbytery is an exercise in grace and symmetry, and incorporates one of Scotland's finest examples of the 'Perpendicular' style of tracery – the delicate stonework of the window. Above this, a carved group of seated figures represents the Coronation of the Virgin Mary. On either side are statues, one a cleric with his mitre. Cross-legged figures of men or women perch on the slopes of the buttresses.

The windows in the south transept and the two eastern nave chapels are probably the work of John Morow, and show a debt to French styles in their restrained forms. Large buttresses support the aisle chapels, on the south side of the church. Amongst the carvings, a shield bears the royal arms of James IV, dated 1505. Beneath the shield, another once displayed the arms of Abbot William Turnbull. On either side are a mason's mell, or mallet, and a rose – a rebus on the name Melrose. This play on words is repeated on an adjacent buttress.

In a niche high on the westernmost buttress is a replica figure of the Virgin and Child. The original sculpture is conserved in the abbey collections. The abbey church at Melrose, like all Cistercian houses, was dedicated to St Mary the Virgin. This statue is positioned, in alignment with the *pulpitum*, at the western limit of the monks' choir. The Virgin is defaced and the Child is headless. Even so, the effigy is one of the finest pieces of medieval figure-sculpture surviving in Scotland. The Virgin is veiled and crowned and her robes drape in well-balanced folds. She supports the child with her left arm, and holds a flower in her right hand. The canopy over her head and the corbel beneath her feet are elaborately carved.

In the niche of the next buttress is St Andrew, now very defaced. The statue was not designed to fit the niche, and may have been brought here from elsewhere in the church. Look above for two gargoyles, or water-spouts; one depicts a winged, calf-headed beast, while the other is Melrose's famous carving of a musical pig.

Opposite: The arms of James IV, dated 1505. Though now much worn, carvings on either side of the bottom shield played on the name Melrose.

Top: The original Virgin and Child statue, now conserved in the abbey collections.

Bottom: How James IV's arms (opposite) may have looked before the carving was eroded.

THE CHAPTER HOUSE

The chapter house was the monks' main meeting room. They met here every morning, to hear a chapter from the Rule of St Benedict, to confess misdemeanours, and to discuss business matters.

This was also a favoured place of burial for abbots and other church dignitaries. Perhaps the most important of these was St Waltheof in 1159. In 1240, a shrine-like tomb was placed over his remains, fragments of which survive and can be seen in the commendator's house.

In addition to ecclesiastical figures, but contrary to the original principles of the Cistercian order, the chapter house became the resting-place for patrons of the abbey.

The *Melrose Chronicle* records several burials, including Philip de Valognes, chamberlain of William I, in 1215, and Christiana Corbet, a relation of the earl of Dunbar, in 1241. Was she perhaps the female skeleton found in a stone coffin in 1921?

Undoubtedly the most intriguing discovery during excavations in 1921 was of a mummified heart enclosed in a lead container. Decomposed iron box straps were found beside it, but nothing to indicate its history. It has been suggested that this was the heart of Robert the Bruce, interred at Melrose in 1331. This seems unlikely. Heart burial was quite common in the medieval period, and it is probable that Bruce's heart was laid to rest in the abbey church beside the high altar. It is possible, though, that some burials were moved when the east end of the church was rebuilt after 1385.

> *The erle off Murreff that had the cur*
> *That tyme off Scotland halely*
> *With gret worschyp has gert bery*
> *The kingis hart at the abbay*
> *Off Melros, quhar men prayis ay*
> *That he and his have paradys.*
>
> From John Barbour's epic poem, *The Brus*, c.1375
>
> 'erle off Murreff' – earl of Moray, 'cur' – care, 'gert' – ordered, 'quhar' – where, 'ay' – ever.

Opposite: The lead casket found in the chapter house in 1921. It was discovered, examined and reburied by archaeologists in 1996.

Above: Stone coffins uncovered during excavations in the chapter house in 1921.

Left: A plinth commemorating Robert the Bruce where the heart casket was discovered. Designed by Victoria Oswald, it is inscribed with a quotation from John Barbour's poem *The Brus*, reading 'A noble hart may have nane ease gif freedom failye.'

THE DOMESTIC BUILDINGS

All that remains today of the chapter house, refectory, dormitory, kitchen and reredorter (or latrine block) are low stone walls, discovered during excavations.

Unusually, at Melrose the monks' living quarters were built to the north of the abbey church. At most abbeys, the cloister and domestic buildings were positioned to the south, where the towering building would not reduce the available daylight. The decision to build on the north here was probably made so that water from the Tweed could be easily diverted and put to good use.

The Cistercian Rule stated that monks should spend their entire day within the church and enclosed world of the cloister. At the centre of the cloister was an open rectangular space, or garth, probably laid out as a garden.

Around the garth were four covered alleys where monks worked, and which sheltered them as they passed between buildings. The surviving walls of the cloister have stone benches and elaborate wall arcades.

Off the east alley were the most important rooms. Closest to the church was the chapter house. Beside it was probably the inner parlour, where necessary conversation was permitted; for much of the time the brethren were silent.

At the end of the range was a room with a vaulted ceiling, supported by a central row of columns. This was probably the novices' day room, where those who had not yet taken vows were initiated into the monastic way of life. At right angles to these buildings was the reredorter, or latrine block, serving the monks' dormitory.

The dormitory ran the full length of the east range at first-floor level. To the east there would also have been the monks' infirmary, a fragment of which may survive in the masons' work yard.

Projecting from the centre of the north alley was the refectory, or dining hall, where the monks ate in silence.

Right: An artist's impression of Melrose Abbey in around 1500.

Left: The remains of the *lavatorium*, where monks washed before dining in the refectory.

It was originally built parallel to the north walk, but in the 1200s was rebuilt at right angles to it, probably to create a much larger space. The *lavatorium*, or wash place, was directly opposite the refectory entrance.

Here monks would wash their hands in a great circular basin, fed with water brought in lead pipes from a well to the south of the abbey. The kitchen was next to the refectory.

THE DOMESTIC BUILDINGS (CONTINUED)

The abbey precinct at Melrose was unusually large, and would have been bustling with abbey business.

Off the west walk of the cloister lived the lay brothers, in their own buildings. The remains are the most complicated in the entire abbey complex, as the lay brothers had all the same needs as the monks – dormitory, dining room, infirmary etc – but also needed work spaces. The remains of these buildings are hard to read. A fireplace in the west wall indicates the site of their warming house. The north block had a central line of pillars. The south block may have started as the refectory, but was later converted into workshops. Three leather tanning pits survive today. There must once also have been a bake house and brew house, but the remains are possibly lost or covered by the road.

Near the tanning pits stands the commendator's house. Originally built in the 1400s for an unknown purpose, it contained at least three rooms on the ground floor, each with a hooded fireplace. The upper rooms were entered from a timber gallery, reached by an outside stair. In 1590 James Douglas, the last commendator of the abbey, converted it into his house.

The gallery was removed and the square stair-tower was added at the corner. Vaulted cellars and a kitchen were inserted in the ground floor and the upper floors reorganised. The building now houses one of the finest collections of objects and architectural fragments from any ecclesiastical site in Britain, some of them found in the main drain.

Not far from the commendator's house you can see the foundations of what was probably the abbot's hall. The *Melrose Chronicle* for 1246 records that Abbot Matthew erected a magnificent hall on the bank of the stream together with many convenient offices.

Next to this is the mill-lade, which is fed from a dam across the Tweed, a quarter of a mile west of the abbey.

STAIRWAY TO HEAVEN

Lay brothers were usually illiterate men from modest backgrounds who took vows of poverty, chastity and obedience. They lived in the monastery in order to perform manual work. In the early days of the Cistercian order, their manual labour was seen as offering as straight a path to God as the prayer and study of the monks themselves.

Above: A lay brother depicted in a monastic account book of the 1270s.

Opposite: Pits where skins or hides were tanned to make leather in the abbey's later years.

Top left: The Commendator's House.

A HEAVENLY PLACE

The Cistercians often favoured a river valley location for their monasteries, and Melrose is no exception. The flat, fertile land of the Tweed valley and the surrounding uplands were key to sustaining monastic life and generating income.

When the monastery was established by David I in 1136, it was supplied with the land between the Tweed and the Eildon Hills to the south of the precinct. The position of the river north of the site led the monks to build their cloister to the north of the church (rather than the lighter south). This allowed buildings such as the infirmary and kitchens, which needed an ample supply of water, to be closer to the river.

Part of the river was diverted through the precinct where it first flowed to the buildings which needed clean water, before being used to power the monks' water mill and flush their latrine.

The monks used the land around the monastery to grow crops, and to graze their animals. Wool was the most important source of income for Melrose and the hills around the abbey were perfect for grazing their flocks, but they also kept cattle, and had the right to graze pigs on the King's land north of the river. He had also granted them the right to fish in the river, and to take wood from his forests at Selkirk and Traquair. As the monastery's land-holdings in the area grew in the centuries after its foundation, the monks acquired more land of their own to the north of the Tweed. The arable and livestock products of the abbey's land would be brought to farm buildings close to the abbey to be processed.

Fruit flourished in the temperate climate of the Borders, including the apple known as the White Melrose.

First described in 1813, it is believed to have been bred by the monks themselves. The apple is still grown today and is suitable for both cooking and eating. In 1884 the area was known as being 'a splendid district for fruit, especially in the immediate vicinity of Melrose Abbey'. Priorwood Garden, run by the National Trust for Scotland, continues the tradition of apple-growing in the abbey precinct, probably on the site of the monastic kitchen garden.

The wildlife around the abbey has changed little down the centuries. The flat marshy ground close to Melrose is a good place to see black-headed gulls and a variety of waterfowl, while red squirrels have been repopulating the region in the past few years.

Right: A red squirrel.

Above: The White Melrose apple.

Opposite: Melrose Abbey, lying in the valley of the river Tweed, surrounded by hills.

THE HISTORY OF MELROSE ABBEY

In the mid-600s, St Aidan of Lindisfarne established a monastery at 'Mailros', which would become a renowned place of godliness and learning.

Centuries later, Cistercian monks built a monastery only two and a half miles away, inspired by the site's holy history.

From its foundation in 1136 to the day the last monk died in 1590, the great abbey church of St Mary the Virgin dominated this fertile border valley. The great and good endowed it, and a hallowed few were buried here, including Alexander II in 1249 and the heart of Robert the Bruce in 1331.

It attracted unwanted attention from the English during the Wars of Independence. The present rose-stoned abbey church dates almost entirely from a rebuilding campaign which followed a devastating raid by Richard II's army in 1385. It survives to this day as a marvel of medieval architecture.

This page: The town and abbey of Melrose, painted by I Clark in 1825.

OLD MELROSE

A little to the east of Melrose, within a loop of the winding River Tweed, is a secluded spot now called Old Melrose. It is here that Melrose's story truly begins shortly before the year 650.

At this time, St Aidan of Lindisfarne established a monastery here, bringing monks from the Columban monastery on Iona. 'Mailros' lay within the kingdom of Northumbria, and its first abbot, Eata, was one of 12 Saxon youths taught by Aidan. Mailros's most famous son was St Cuthbert. He entered the monastery after having a vision whilst shepherding on the Lammermuir Hills, apparently on the very night St Aidan died in 651. The youth, who had loved games and pranks, in time succeeded Boisil as prior of Mailros and in 664 became prior of Lindisfarne.

Right: The site of Old Melrose, lying in a loop of the winding River Tweed. The Eildon Hills are in the distance.

TIMELINE

698

ST CUTHBERT'S tomb is opened, and his body found to be incorrupt.

850

KENNETH MACALPIN leads the Scots to conquer the borders. Old Melrose is destroyed in the process.

St Aidan – An Irish monk, who became known as the Apostle of Northumbria. He travelled through the country to spread God's word to the noble and the poor. He founded monasteries at Lindisfarne and Mailros, and died in 651.

St Boisil – The first prior of Mailros, after whom the nearby village of St Boswells is named. He was known for his miraculous visions. When St Cuthbert first approached Mailros, Boisil foresaw his future greatness, and told his companions to 'Behold the servant of the Lord'.

St Cuthbert – Boisil's student, Cuthbert became one of the most important medieval saints. As prior of Mailros and Lindisfarne, he advised on spiritual matters, spread the word of God and performed miracles. He died while living as a hermit on the island of Inner Farne in 687. Durham Cathedral was founded in veneration of him after his death.

Above: Boisil welcomes Cuthbert into the abbey of Mailros, from Bede's *Life of St Cuthbert*.

Two centuries later the abbey that Cuthbert knew was destroyed by the Scots, who were fighting the Northumbrians for control of the region. The sanctity of the place lived on, though, and between 1073–5 it was a retreat for Prior Turgot of Durham, later confessor and chronicler to St Margaret of Scotland. A church of sorts seems to have continued at Old Melrose into the 1200s.

Little is known of the planning of these early monasteries, but at Old Melrose the boundary is visible, a ditch, or *vallum*, cutting off the neck of the promontory on which the monastery stood. At the heart of the monastery would have been the church and around it the individual cells of the monks, their granaries, storehouses, workshops and guestrooms.

THE CISTERCIANS

' Our food is scanty, our garments rough; our drink is from the stream and our sleep is often upon our book. Under our tired limbs there is but a hard mat; when sleep is sweetest we must rise at bell's bidding... Everywhere peace, everywhere serenity and a marvellous freedom from the tumult of the world.'
Abbot Aelred of Rievaulx

Cistercian monasticism was established in 1098 at Citeaux, near Dijon in Burgundy. It was one of several attempts to return an increasingly indulgent monastic system to the strict Rule of St Benedict.

The rise of the order was meteoric despite its uncompromising insistence on poverty, austerity and labour. The first Cistercian house in Britain was founded in 1128 at Waverley, Surrey.

Rievaulx followed three years later, and was the mother house of both Melrose, in 1136, and Dundrennan, in Galloway, in 1142. Nine more Scottish Cistercian houses followed; the last was Sweetheart Abbey in Galloway, as late as 1273.

The order deliberately settled in remote places, 'far from the concourse of men'. Its lands and industries were worked solely by and for the community. They achieved this through the use of 'lay brothers'. These men lived a cloistered life, but undertook a greater part of the manual labour at the expense of the religious life. They were permitted longer sleep and more food for their pains.

The monks and lay brothers wore undyed woollen habits and became commonly known as 'the white monks'. Beneath their habits they wore no undershirts or woollen breeches — even in the chilly hills of Scotland. Their diet was strictly vegetarian, but wholesome.

The Cistercian life revolved around the daily church offices, with the remainder of the day occupied by work, sleep or private prayer. The abbot was assisted by the prior (his deputy), the precentor, who arranged the church services, the cellarer, who kept the abbey supplied, and the almoner, who ministered to the poor. Links with the outside world were restricted to the abbot and principal office holders, who were often absent on business, and the lay brethren, who staffed the outlying granges or sheep farms for part of their time.

Below: Cistercians praying over a monk's body, depicted in a Book of Hours of the later 1300s.

Right: A French funeral mass of the early 1400s. Cistercian monks sit in choir stalls, with five spectral figures in the back row.

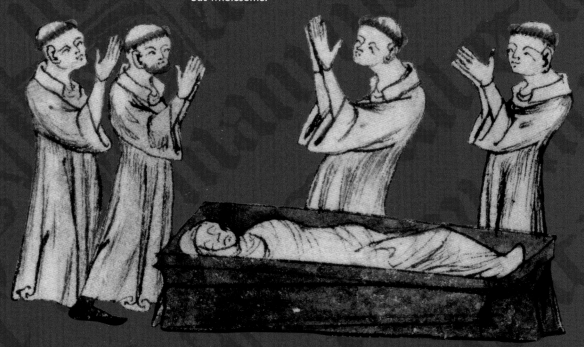

DAVID I'S ABBEY

When David I invited Cistercian monks from Rievaulx Abbey in Yorkshire to set up their first house in Scotland in 1136, he chose Old Melrose as their site. The monks clearly found it unsuitable and moved a little further west to a place called Little Fordell – now Melrose itself.

David I liberally endowed the abbey, and encouraged others to do likewise. The monks received land as far away as Ayrshire, property in towns such as Berwick and Edinburgh, and other assets in the form of fishing rights, salt-marshes and peat-bogs. Such was Melrose's popularity that it became one of Britain's wealthiest monasteries.

It was also held in great regard. David I's step-son, Waltheof, the second abbot, was famed for performing miracles. After his death, his fame grew, and may have attracted wealthy and noble men to the church.

Both Robert Avenel, lord of Eskdale, and Richard de Moreville, high constable of Scotland, enrolled as novices there in later life.

The 13 monks arriving from Rievaulx (Abbot Richard and 12 others, mirroring Christ and his disciples) began building their new abbey in strict accordance with Cistercian Rule. They therefore started constructing the church's east end first. By 1146, the work was sufficiently advanced for a dedication service to take place.

Building work would continue for the next 50 years.

Little of the first church is now visible, but excavation has identified the main elements of the plan. It follows closely that of Rievaulx, which in turn was probably modelled on its mother house of Clairvaux, the Cistercians' house in eastern France. The simplicity of the architecture for which the Cistercians were renowned at this date is evident in the surviving west wall (pages 8–9).

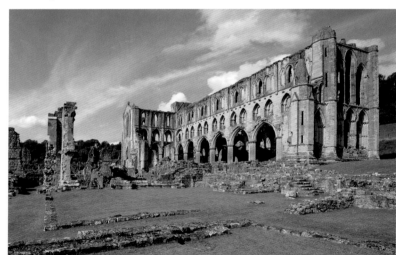

1136

DAVID I
invites monks from Rievaulx to set up a monastery at Melrose.

1159

ST WALTHEOF
abbot of Melrose, dies and comes to be considered a saint.

WALTHEOF, THE SAINTLY ABBOT OF MELROSE

And rejoice in the Lord all you monks of Melrose, who, already drenched with honey and heavenly dew, have with you your honey-sweet father before your eyes, more like a man sleeping than dead.

Walter Bower in 15th-century *Scotichronicon*

Of noble birth, St Waltheof rose quickly through the ranks of the Augustinian order, before entering the Cistercian order as a monk. He became abbot of Melrose, and is said to have performed many miracles. In 1171 his tomb was opened and 'his body was found entire, and his vestments intact, in the twelfth year from his death'. Again in 1206, a mason working on a new tomb cover peeped inside, and saw that the body had not decayed. In 1240, a few small bones were removed as relics for pilgrims to venerate and be cured. Fragments of his shrine, discovered in 1921, are displayed in the commendator's house.

Below: Fragments of Waltheof's tomb – now on display in the Commendator's House.

Above: David I, shown on the Kelso Charter of 1159.

Opposite: Rievaulx Abbey in North Yorkshire, from which monks travelled north to found an abbey at Melrose in 1136.

MONASTIC LIFE AT MELROSE

'Give the Cistercians a wilderness or forest and in a few years you will find a dignified abbey in the midst of plenty.'
Bishop Gerald of Wales, 1188

Alongside their duties in the church, the monks of Melrose performed a range of activities within the cloister and the wider precinct during their working day.

Apart from their principal activity of offering prayer, reading and writing were among the most important tasks of the monastic community, so much so that Richard, the first Abbot of Melrose, wrote that 'a cloister without literature is a grave for living men'. Time each day was set aside for private study, especially during Lent when the Rule of St Benedict placed a special emphasis on reading and contemplation.

The monks at Melrose also spent some time compiling their chronicle. Although about 20 Cistercian houses in the British Isles kept chronicles, the one at Melrose was probably the oldest: it was kept updated from 1173-4 until the early 1300s. Under a heading for each year, a scribe would record important events at the local, national and international level. Although the content varied over time, the Chronicle recorded largely the appointment, resignation or death of ecclesiastical personnel; the deeds of the kings of Scotland, England and France as well as the Popes; and some items referring to the day-to-day life of the monastery such as their property rights. They also backdated the chronicle to record events as far back as the birth of Christ, although the years 250-730 have been lost. Today the *Melrose Chronicle* survives in two manuscripts, both held by the British Library in London.

As well as working on manuscripts within the cloister, the monks also managed their extensive farms. During the first centuries of the monastery's life these farms were worked by the lay brothers. By the 1400s, recruitment of lay brothers had dwindled to almost nothing. The monks then rented out many of their farms, while servants did much of the work around the monastery itself.

The most important product of Melrose Abbey was wool – one of Scotland's largest exports in the medieval period. As well as raising and shearing sheep, the monastery graded and processed their wool ready for export, and took it to Berwick-upon-Tweed where they had property in which to store it, and their own ship in which to transport it. The abbey probably also processed and transported wool for smaller Cistercian monasteries which may not have had such resources.

By the mid-1300s, when wool production was at its height in Scotland, Melrose owned around 17,000 sheep and was important enough to be named as a major Scottish producer by the Italian merchant Francesco Balducci Pegolotti in a guide he wrote to successful trade. Monasteries had a number of advantages over other merchants when selling their wool: they did not have to pay tolls when they travelled on the road, and many Cistercian houses secured tax concessions on their wool exports. In the 1180s, for example, the court of Flanders granted the monks of Melrose exemption from tolls. As a result, they could make a significant profit which they used to improve their monastery.

Right: A novice and monk of Cîteaux Abbey fell a tree, in a manuscript dating to 1111.

Opposite: Cistercian monks harvesting wheat, on an Austrian altar panel of around 1500.

THE WARS OF INDEPENDENCE

> *One monk, who was infirm, and two blind lay brothers, were killed by the same Englishmen in their dormitory, and many monks were fatally wounded. The Body of Christ was flung on to the high altar when the silver pyx in which it was kept was stolen.*
>
> Walter Bower, on the sacking of Melrose in 1322

The first 200 years of abbey life passed peacefully, disturbed only by construction work and numerous land disputes. But this tranquility was shattered when Edward I of England invaded Scotland in 1296.

Melrose, at the heart of the Border country, was to suffer repeated damage for the next 250 years. Shortly after the outbreak of the wars with England, Abbot Patrick swore an oath of allegiance to Edward I at Berwick, and evidence shows that Melrose was considered important by the English authorities.

In 1305, the abbot was amongst those named as Scottish commissioners to the English parliament for drawing up the settlement for the future government of Scotland. The monks also let out some of their storage space – 15 granaries and four cellars held surplus grain from the English supply base at Berwick.

This relationship deteriorated after Robert the Bruce declared himself king in 1306. By 1314, Bruce had re-captured Roxburgh Castle for the Scots, and gained firm control over Teviotdale.

Two years later, Bruce himself was based at Melrose, and it was from here that he launched raids into English-held lands. In 1322 Edward II's army sacked the abbey.

Robert the Bruce helped fund the rebuilding work. After his death, Bruce's heart was carried on crusade by his friend, the Good Sir James of Douglas. Sir James died fighting the Moors in Spain, and in 1331, Bruce's heart was returned to Scotland and buried at Melrose Abbey, his body having been interred in Dunfermline Abbey.

Right: Robert the Bruce, who launched raids against the English from his base in Melrose during the Wars of Independence.

1296

EDWARD I
of England invades Scotland, beginning the Wars of Independence.

1385

RICHARD II
of England's soldiers destroy much of Melrose Abbey.

Below: Edward III of England and David II of Scotland make peace in the 1357 Treaty of Berwick, ending the Wars of Independence.

In 1357, David II returned to Scotland after long imprisonment in England. An uneasy peace returned to the Borders. But in 1385 the Scots invaded England. The English retaliated, and the soldiers of 19-year-old Richard II of England devastated the eastern Borders.

The 15th-century *Scotichronicon* relates how they 'burnt to ashes with consuming flames churches devoted to God and monastic sanctuaries (namely the monasteries at Dryburgh, Melrose and Newbattle)'.

The monks looked at their smoking ruin and decided there was nothing for it but to rebuild anew. For the next 100 years and more, the masons worked to create what remains a masterpiece of medieval architecture. The Cistercians had moved a long way from the simple aspirations of their founders.

A PHOENIX FROM THE ASHES

The rebuilding work at the abbey began almost immediately. The style of the resulting architecture tells a tale of political unrest and shifting cultural allegiances.

The abbey financed the rebuilding at least partly from customs exemptions on their wool exports, granted from both the Scottish and English kings. In 1386, Robert II of Scotland granted them an exemption on customs for all of their own wool. This continued to make money for the abbey into the later 1400s. In 1389, Richard II of England too granted Melrose favourable export terms – an abatement of two shillings a sack on the customs charge on Scottish wool exported through Berwick, for up to 1,000 sacks. This was over 20 times the amount of wool produced by the abbey itself, so they must have been acting as an agent for other Scottish wool producers.

However, it seems that the monks sought to capitalise on Richard's generous terms, and tried to export 200 sacks over their allowance. Richard cancelled his abatement after only a year.

By the 1390s, Melrose lay once again within Scottish jurisdiction. In the building work, a shift of style reflects the bitter relations between Scotland and England. For the first stages of rebuilding, during which the scale and floor plan of the new cathedral were determined, English masons seem to have directed the operation. But responsibility for the building work soon shifted. There is a distinct change in style, most obviously in the south transept and the south aisle chapels. Here the more flowing forms of the window tracery have been inspired by European buildings, and two inscriptions in the south transept record that this particular part of the work was supervised by the French master-mason, John Morow (page 14).

The rebuilding work continued through the 1400s and into the 1500s. James IV distributed drink-silver to the masons during his visits in 1502 and 1504. The church was probably never fully completed, with the western parts of the first church perhaps never being replaced by the intended new work. But even in its unfinished state it must have been magnificent to behold. While today's visitor has only the splendour of the masonry to admire, gleaming metalwork, finely crafted furnishings, and coloured floor tiles once filled the spaces of this great church.

Opposite: The east end of Melrose Abbey – an exercise in grace and symmetry – painted by Robert Billings in 1832.

1386

ROBERT II
grants Melrose tax concessions, enabling the monks to raise money to rebuild the abbey.

1400

JOHN MOROW
French master mason, creates flowing designs in the south transept at Melrose.

john:morow:fum:tym:callit :
was:..and:born:in:parpffe :
certanlu:and:had:in:kepyng :
al : mafon:werk:of:fantan
drous:ve:hve:kyrk:of:glaf
gw:melros:and:pallau: of:
nuddufdaull:and:of:gallwau:
f:pray:to:god:and:mari:bathe:
a:fweete:fanct:johne:to:kepe:
this:halu:kyrk:fra:fkathe :

DECLINE AND FALL

By the time of the Protestant Reformation in 1560, more than the church's architecture had changed at Melrose.

The economy continued to revolve around sales of wool, now produced by tenant farmers rather than by lay brothers. Abbots were frequently absent on affairs of state, leaving control of the monastery to their priors. Abbot Andrew Hunter, for example, was James II's treasurer in 1450.

The dilution of strict Cistercian Rule is evident in a ruling made by the abbots of Coupar Angus and Glenluce in 1534. They decreed that the monks of Melrose must cease keeping private lodgings and gardens. A compromise was reached, allowing the gardens to continue, but declaring that the produce must be used communally.

Opposite above: John Slezer's 1693 engraving of 'The Ruines of the Abbie of Melross'.

Opposite below: 'The monks of Melrose made gude kail' by Charles Landseer.

Another sign of decline was the appointment in 1535 of James V's 5-year-old son, James Stewart, as commendator, or administrator of the abbey. By 1539 only 22 monks were left.

In the mid-1500s, Melrose was again touched by war. James V's death in 1542 placed his infant daughter Mary on the throne. This led to the 'Rough Wooing' – an attempt by England's Henry VIII to force a marriage between Mary and his son Edward. In 1544 the English set fire to Melrose's church and desecrated the tombs. In 1545 the Battle of Ancrum Moor was fought nearby. When the English commander Sir Ralph Evers was killed, he was buried in the church he had looted a year earlier.

The abbey buildings fell into disrepair. In 1556, the monks warned that 'without the kirk be repairit this instant sommer God service will ceise this winter'. Four years later, the Protestant Reformation officially abolished Catholic worship in Scotland.

The remaining monks lived out their days at the abbey, still receiving their 'portions' of monastic income. In 1573 Sir Walter Scott of Branxholm was accused of dismantling 'the inner queir' [the monks' choir], the 'uter kirk' [the nave], 'the stepile and croce kirk of the same' [the tower and transepts] and carrying off the stones, timber, lead, iron and glass. Soon after 1590, the last monk – John Watson, described as 'only convent' – passed away.

About 1610, the monks' choir was converted for use as a parish church. The last commendator, James Douglas, created a residence in what is now known as the 'commendator's house'. Douglas resigned and, in 1608, the abbey lands were sold. Melrose passed through the hands of the earls of Haddington, to be bought by Anne, Duchess of Buccleuch, widow of the executed 1st Duke of Monmouth. In 1810, a new parish church was built in the town, and over 1,000 years of worship at Melrose came to an end.

1542

JAMES V
dies. His infant daughter, Mary, becomes Queen of Scots at only six days old.

1560

JOHN KNOX
leads the Protestant Reformation in Scotland. Catholic worship comes to an end at Melrose.

'The monks of Melrose
made gude kail
on Fridays when they fasted;
nor wanted they gude beef and ale,
as lang's their neighbour's lasted.'

Snippet of an old ballad, satirising
the relaxed nature of monastic life
at Melrose.

'FAR-FAM'D GLORIOUS RUINS'

> *'If thou wouldn't view fair Melrose aright*
> *Go visit it by pale moonlight;*
> *For the gay beams of lightsome day*
> *Gild, but to flount the ruins grey.'*
>
> Sir Walter Scott,
> *Lay of the Last Minstrel*, 1805.

By the later 1700s, melancholy ruins and picturesque decay were very much in fashion. Images of moonlit Melrose became very popular. In 1789, the poet Robert Burns visited the abbey, and was charmed by its 'far-fam'd glorious ruins'.

The growing national appreciation for the buildings induced its owner, the 3rd Duke of Buccleuch, to agree to pay for the conservation of the abbey church, once it had been vacated by the parish congregation – a key factor in their relocation to a new church in 1810 and the survival of the abbey buildings.

From the later 1700s onwards, the romantic abbey ruins inspired poets and artists of international fame, helping to ensure the preservation of the buildings for posterity.

After the Protestant Reformation, monastic buildings were publicly reviled for the way of life they represented. As time moved on, though, appreciation for medieval craftsmanship grew. Certainly, when John Slezer recorded monuments of Scotland in his 1693 volume *Theatrum Scotiae*, the architecture of Melrose was carefully and delicately drawn.

Right: The abbey depicted in Sir Walter Scott's *Antiquities of the Scottish Border*, 1814.

1769

HENRY SCOTT
3rd Duke of Buccleuch, commissions a series of views of Melrose. He later funds conservation work at the abbey.

1919

JOHN MONTAGU DOUGLAS SCOTT
7th Duke of Buccleuch, hands Melrose Abbey into State care.

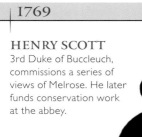

Above: Tourists explore the presbytery, in a painting of 1811 by F.J. Sarjent.

The abbey ruins were preserved thanks to their enlightened and wealthy owner. But some of the credit also lies at the door of the abbey's near neighbour, Sir Walter Scott. His decision to build his Baronial dream house nearby – taking direct architectural inspiration from the abbey – brought many tourists to the area.

Scott's personal affection for Melrose was clear – indeed, he named his new home Abbotsford, in reference to the ford where the monks were said to have crossed the River Tweed. The site he chose was formerly known as Cartleyhole (or satirically Clarty Hole, for its muddy location).

Scott also included the abbey in many of his novels and poems, and Melrose became known to an ever wider public.

J.M.W. Turner illustrated the abbey for Scott's *Lay of Last Minstrel*, and Melrose was placed firmly on the billing for any tour of Scotland.

After Scott's death in 1832, the abbey was one of the chief inspirations for the architecture of the Scott Monument in Edinburgh, designed by George Meikle Kemp. It has continued to play an important role in Scottish culture and design ever since. The abbey itself was handed into State care in 1919.

Melrose Abbey is one of many Historic Scotland sites in the Scottish Borders, a selection of which is shown below.

JEDBURGH ABBEY

Explore one of four great abbeys built in the Scottish Borders in the 1100s. Built over more than 70 years, Jedburgh is striking for its unusual mix of architectural styles.

↗ In Jedburgh on A68

🕐 Open all year

📞 01835 863 925

🚗 Approx. **13 miles** from Melrose Abbey

DRYBURGH ABBEY

Wander among the tranquil, tree-lined ruins of the medieval abbey, on the banks of the River Tweed. Don't miss the surviving paint and plaster in the chapter house.

↗ On B6404 near St Boswells

🕐 Open all year

📞 01835 822 381

🚗 Approx. **7 miles** from Melrose Abbey

SMAILHOLM TOWER

This Borders stronghold of the 1400s towers 20 metres tall on a craggy outcrop. It inspired Walter Scott's interest in Border Ballads, and plays a starring role in some of his poetry.

↗ In Smailholm village, 6m west of Kelso on the A6089

🕐 Open summer only

📞 01573 460 365

🚗 Approx. **9 miles** from Melrose Abbey

HERMITAGE CASTLE

Discover a history of intrigue, murder and treason. For centuries this awesome, eerie ruin was a border fortress, and 'the guardhouse of the bloodiest valley in Britain'.

↗ On the B6399, NE of Newcastleton

🕐 Open summer only

📞 01387 376 222

🚗 Approx. **36 miles** from Melrose Abbey

For more information on all Historic Scotland sites, visit **www.historicenvironment.scot**

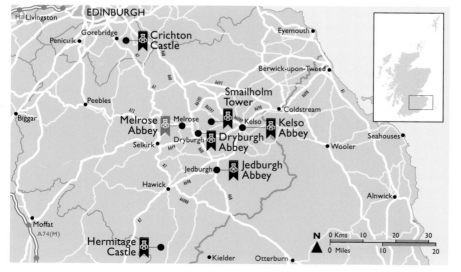

Car parking	🅿
Bus parking	🅿
Reasonable wheelchair access	♿
Interpretive display	
Shop	🛍
Tea/coffee facilities	☕
Accessible by public transport	
Restaurant/café	🍽
Picnic area	
Disabled toilet	♿
Toilets	🚻
Guided tours	
Sturdy footwear recommended	👟
Visitor centre	𝑖
No dogs allowed	🚫